Muslims, Christians, and Jesus

PARTICIPANT'S GUIDE

Muslims, Christians, and Jesus

Gaining Understanding and Building Relationships

PARTICIPANT'S GUIDE
Four Sessions

CARL MEDEARIS

with Stephen & Amanda Sorenson

ZONDERVAN®

ZONDERVAN.com/
AUTHORTRACKER
follow your favorite authors

ZONDERVAN

Muslims, Christians, and Jesus Participant's Guide
Copyright © 2011 by Carl Medearis

Requests for information should be addressed to:
Zondervan, *Grand Rapids, Michigan 49530*

ISBN 978-0-310-89086-7

Cover design: Dan Pitts
Cover photography: Nicole Gibson, www.nicolegibsonphotography.com
Interior design: Sherri L. Hoffman

Printed in the United States of America

11 12 13 14 15 16 /DCI/ 23 22 21 20 19 18 17 16 15 14 13 12 11 10 9 8 7 6 5 4 3 2 1

CONTENTS

INTRODUCTION

A shadow has fallen over many of us who seek to follow Jesus. Not only do we wonder if Muslims are safe enough to reach out to, but we struggle to have the compassion of Christ to do so. It's easy to believe that the problem is Islam itself. For centuries, many people have reduced the conflict to a simplistic generalization: *Christianity vs. Islam*.

There is no doubt that religion can be a hotbed for deep convictions, zealous emotions, and, at times, fiery conflicts. While it is true that some terrorists today utilize the banner of Islam to kill and destroy, there is nothing to be gained by accusing a religion of brokering violence when it is committed by a handful of its followers. I am convinced that the majority of Muslims are far more concerned with obeying the commandments of God than waging holy war against infidels. In fact, I have observed many Muslims who already live close to the truths of Jesus.

Therefore, my intention through this study is to help those who follow Jesus to focus less on whether or not it is "safe" to reach out to Muslims and more on the clear command of Christ to "go into *all* the world." This is a topic I first explored in my book, *Muslims, Christians, and Jesus*, published by Bethany House. I am grateful to Bethany for allowing me to use that book as a foundation to develop the *Muslims, Christians, and Jesus* video curriculum.

I highly recommend reading the original book *Muslims, Christians, and Jesus* as you progress through this study. It offers many more stories of how Muslims have grown in their relationship with Jesus. It helps you to answer common questions Muslims ask. It shows practical ways to love your neighbor by reaching out to Muslims.

I'm not the final word on Islam. I'm only a follower of Jesus who loves Muslims and seeks to live out his command to go into *all* the world. My desire is to introduce you to practical steps you can take to befriend a Muslim. I want to show you how to avoid making stereotypes of Muslims and to avoid reinforcing stereotypes of Christians. I want to help you learn how to live a life that truly is good news to a Muslim.

Carl Medearis
Denver, Colorado
April 2011

HOW TO USE THIS GUIDE

Group Size

The *Muslims, Christians, and Jesus* video curriculum is designed to be experienced in a group setting such as a Bible study, Sunday school class, or any small group gathering. To ensure everyone has enough time to participate in discussions, it is recommended that large groups break up into smaller groups of four to six people each.

Materials Needed

Each participant should have his or her own participant's guide, which includes video outline notes, group discussion questions, personal reflection, informative sidebars, as well as a "Steps to Take on Your Own" activity section to deepen learning between sessions. Although the course can be fully experienced with just the video and participant's guide, participants are also encouraged to have a copy of the *Muslims, Christians, and Jesus* book. Reading the book alongside the video curriculum provides deeper insights that make the journey richer and more meaningful.

Timing

The time notations—for example *(20 minutes)*—indicate the *actual* time of video segments and the *suggested* time for other activities or discussions. For example:

DVD DISCUSSION

(7 minutes)

Adhering to the suggested times will enable you to complete each session in one hour. If you have additional time, you may wish to allow more time for discussion and activities.

Facilitation

Each group should appoint a facilitator who is responsible for starting the video and keeping track of time during discussions and activities. Facilitators may also read questions aloud and monitor discussions, prompting participants to respond and ensuring that everyone has the opportunity to participate. For ease of use, Bible passages are printed in the participant's guide.

Before You Begin

Prior to Session 1, it will be helpful for you to view the "10 Myths about Muslims" and "For Leaders" segments on the DVD.

Of Note

Quotations throughout this participant's guide are taken or adapted from Carl Medearis's book, *Muslims, Christians, and Jesus* (Bethany House, 2008), and are so noted. For brevity, the book title has been abbreviated *MCJ*.

SESSION 1

What Is Islam?: Exploring Our Fears and Stereotypes

How are those of us who follow Jesus supposed to relate to Muslims? This is not a question about differences between the religions of Christianity and Islam, nor is it about political distinctions between the Muslim world and the West. It is, rather, a question of the heart. How do we express an attitude of love and compassion toward people we don't understand? How do we reach out to people who follow an unfamiliar religion that most of us find intimidating? How do we deal with our fear and suspicion so that we might begin to build bridges that lead to Jesus, the Prince of Peace?

MCJ

LET'S THINK ABOUT IT

(4 minutes)

The centuries-long history of conflict between Christianity and Islam has led to negative perceptions, fears, and emotionally charged interactions between people of both faiths today. Even the words we use to talk about these religions and their respective beliefs or practices can incite a spontaneous, powerful response.

- For example, what do you think and feel when you read or hear words such as: *infidel, Crusades, Islam, jihad, Sharia, Christian?*
- What do you think a Muslim might think and feel regarding these same words?

DVD OBSERVATIONS

(20 minutes)

As you watch the video segment for this session, use the following topics as a guide for taking notes.

Islam and Christianity: the roots of our fear

John 4:35 — Open your eyes

    to God's love for all people

    to those who are hungry to hear the good news of Jesus

The language of the Qur'an

The voices of Islam — political violence vs. moderation

What message might Muslims be open to hearing?

DVD DISCUSSION

1. When the tensions that often exist between Christians and Muslims were explored in the video, what did you think and feel? Why?

2. In what ways have various influences (such as culture, news media, church teaching, your family, where you have lived, personal relationships, and your formal education) shaped your perceptions of Islam and Muslims?

    To what extent have your perceptions affected your willingness to learn more about Islam and its followers?

3. When definitions of key words such as *infidel, jihad*, and *Sharia* were explained in the video, how did they compare to your understanding of those words and your view of Muslims?

4.   What do you think it would be like to be a Muslim who lives, works, and raises a family in your community today?

If you were a Muslim living in your community, what might be your view of Americans? Or Christians?

What might you fear?

5.   What kind of relationship do you think Jesus wants his followers to have with Muslims?

GROUP BIBLE EXPLORATION

(18 minutes)

What Does Jesus See?

Jesus clearly viewed the world from a different perspective. While Jesus lived and taught on earth, his viewpoint and responses to what was happening in the world around him often surprised people. He reached out to bless little children instead of shooing them away. He challenged some of the closely held practices of the religious establishment. At times his teachings amazed his disciples, and at other times they struggled to understand his meaning.

1. Jesus' unique perspective is clearly seen in his encounter with the Samaritan woman at the well (John 4:1 – 42). Although Jews and Samaritans normally did not associate with one another, Jesus struck up a conversation with a Samaritan woman whom he knew was an adulterer. He spoke about spiritual matters with such conviction that she ran to gather other people from her village to come and see if he was the Christ!

   a. After his conversation with the Samaritan woman, Jesus said to his disciples: "Open your eyes and look at the fields! They are ripe for harvest. Even now the one who reaps draws a wage and harvests a crop for eternal life, so that the sower and the reaper may be glad together" (John 4:35 – 36). What do you think Jesus was communicating to his disciples by making this statement, and how do you think they understood it?

b. Do you think Jesus' statement means that people today — including Muslims — are ready to receive the good news about Jesus? Why or why not?

2. What Jesus did next is truly amazing: "Many of the Samaritans from that town believed in him because of the woman's testimony, 'He told me everything I ever did.' So when the Samaritans came to him, they urged him to stay with them, and he stayed two days. And because of his words many more became believers. They said to the woman, 'We no longer believe just because of what you said; now we have heard for ourselves, and we know that this man really is the Savior of the world' " (John 4:39 – 42).

a. How badly do you, as a follower of Jesus, want others to know that Jesus really is the Savior of the world? Would you set aside your schedule in order to stay with a person who was hungry to hear about Jesus?

b. What specific actions might followers of Jesus take in order to share who Jesus is with people of other faiths and "harvest" the fields that Jesus says are ripe?

c.   What is holding you back from doing things such as sitting down with a Muslim and beginning a conversation about Jesus?

Jesus Does Not Want Us to Be Afraid

When God calls his people to follow and obey him, fear is a natural response. We do not know what threats may be ahead of us. We do not know what will be required of us or how great the personal cost may be. But God is the God of salvation, not of fear, and throughout the Bible he promises to be with his people when they do his work.

3.   When Joshua assumed leadership of Israel after Moses' death, God told him to "be strong and courageous ... for the LORD your God will be with you wherever you go" (Joshua 1:1 – 9). When Jesus was in a boat with his disciples during a storm on the Sea of Galilee, he calmed the wind and the waves and asked his disciples, "Why are you so afraid? Do you still have no faith?" (Mark 4:40).

a.   What effect do you think fear has on the ability of God's people to fulfill the work he wants to accomplish in the world?

b.   To what extent has our fear of Islam — fueled by a minority who claim their religion as a banner to kill and destroy — convinced us not to reach out to Muslims?

4. At a critical time in Israel's history, God warned the prophet Isaiah: "Do not call conspiracy everything this people call conspiracy; do not fear what they fear, and do not dread it. The LORD Almighty is the one you are to regard as holy, he is the one you are to fear, he is the one you are to dread" (Isaiah 8:12 – 13).

    a. What do people in the West fear about Islam and Muslims?

    b. In what ways do you think this passage can help those of us who follow Jesus today to put our fear of what is happening in the world around us in proper perspective?

5. To help put fear in its proper place, read aloud the following Scripture passages:

    > The LORD is my light and my salvation — whom shall I fear? The LORD is the stronghold of my life — of whom shall I be afraid?
    >
    > Psalm 27:1

    > Do not fear, for I am with you; do not be dismayed, for I am your God. I will strengthen you and help you; I will uphold you with my righteous right hand.
    >
    > Isaiah 41:10

    > Hear me, you who know what is right, you people who have taken my instruction to heart: Do not fear the reproach of mere mortals or be terrified by their insults.... My righteousness will last forever, my salvation through all generations.
    >
    > Isaiah 51:7 – 8

"Do not fear what they fear; do not be frightened." But in your hearts set apart Christ as Lord. Always be prepared to give an answer to everyone who asks you to give the reason for the hope that you have. But do this with gentleness and respect.

1 Peter 3:14–15

a. What do you think causes us to fear sharing the message of Jesus with Muslims, and on what do we need to focus in order to overcome our fear?

b. What are some practical way(s) we might begin to act on our faith and trust in God rather than responding in fear to Muslims?

THINK ABOUT IT

The world is full of strife, war, conflicts, and hatred. The life that Christ offers is the opposite. He provides a way to live in this very world, but to do so in peace and love. But we have to choose his way. It doesn't come easily or naturally.... If you want to reach a [Muslim] person, you have to look at him [or her] as an individual. The preconceptions you may have about Islam need to be discarded from the beginning if you want to have a genuine relationship with a Muslim. There can be no more generalizations and blanket distinctions.... We need to go beyond "understanding" and "dialogue" and get down to a personal heart-to-heart level.

MCJ

Opening Our Hearts to Share the Good News of Jesus

When it comes to Christians and Muslims, it may surprise us that negative stereotypes go both ways! Muslims have judged us the same way that we have judged them. They are just as afraid of us as we are of them. But God wants all the world to know who he is (Isaiah 12:4–6). The love of Christ breaks down the barriers of fear and prejudice and opens our hearts so that we can see, hear, and share the good news that's available to all people.

6. Instead of judging, condemning, and holding grudges, Jesus said: "Do not judge, and you will not be judged. Do not condemn, and you will not be condemned. Forgive, and you will be forgiven" (Luke 6:37).

   a. To what extent have you — and other people you know — feared and judged Muslims based on stereotypes rather than choosing to forgive and reaching out to them?

   b. Why is it important for us as followers of Jesus to examine honestly our tendency to judge and withhold forgiveness from all Muslims because of the harm a few have brought to us?

7. When followers of Jesus consider what it means to obey his clear command to "Go into *all* the world and preach the good news to all creation" (Mark 16:15, italics added), we often wonder if it is "safe" to do so. But that may be the wrong question. The crucial question

is not about whether or not we will be safe, but whether or not we will obey our Savior's command to go and share the good news.

a. In what ways do you think prejudice has led us to focus on the wrong question and hindered us from obeying Jesus' command when it comes to Muslims?

b. How hard is it for us to change our focus and open our hearts with compassion to people who may be just as afraid of us as we are of them?

PERSONAL REFLECTION

As the world watched smoke and ash spew into the Manhattan sky on September 11, 2001, I (Carl) was teaching students in Kansas City about loving Muslims. In fact, I had just drawn a diagram on the white board showing how we so often think in an *us-versus-them* paradigm. I was literally erasing the line between the words *us* and *them* when someone burst into the room in tears and told us what had happened.

The next week, our family returned home to Beirut. For days after our arrival, we received a steady stream of visits and calls from friends saying how sorry they were. One friend, Ahmed (not his real name), came by our house, slumped into our couch, and rubbed his face with his hands.

"Carl," he said, "these terrorists have seriously hurt the peace we have worked so hard for."

"What do you mean?"

"America will go to war," he said, shaking his head, "and I am afraid that it will not end for years."

"I know."

"The West does not understand us. They see an Arab and they feel fear. They hear talk of Islam and they are suspicious. I am afraid that things will spiral out of control and that hatred will grow between my people and your people." He sighed. "Again."

What impact has this session had on your views of Islam and Muslims?

What impact has it had on your willingness to open your eyes to the spiritual harvest that Jesus sees and to open your heart to Muslims?

It doesn't get much press in our world today, but the prophet Muhammad made a treaty with certain Christians in his realm that provided religious and administrative autonomy for non-Muslim citizens of the Islamic State. It allowed, among other things, protection from attack, safe and unhindered worship, and freedom from persecution for the crimes of others. Throughout the centuries, sincere Muslim rulers have adhered to the founding principles of this treaty in managing the affairs of non-Muslim subjects. To learn more, search the Internet for Muhammad's Treaty with the Christians of Najran. Several sources list the details of this pact. One of the most informative sites is Al-Islam.org, which includes an article on foreign policy of an Islamic state by Ibrahim Amini. Part 8 of the article includes Pacts of Cooperation and Non-agression with Unbelievers (www.al-islam.org/al-tawhid/foreign-policy/9.htm).

CLOSING

(1 minute)

Pray about what you have discovered during today's session and how you might apply these discoveries to your life and your relationships with Muslims. Pray especially for a clear understanding of Jesus' example of reaching out to others. Ask God to deliver you from fears that would hinder you from obeying Jesus' command to "go into *all* the world and preach the good news."

STEPS TO TAKE ON YOUR OWN

Each of us has opinions about Islam and Muslims. The events of September 11, 2001 that made terrorism nearly synonymous with Islam have made it easy to cement our stereotypes of Muslims. But fear, anger, bitterness, and/or a lack of forgiveness can quickly cause us to forget how much God loves all people (including Muslims). If our deepest desire is to respond in faith with God's love and to share the good news about Jesus, we need to learn how to reach out and connect heart-to-heart with Muslims and other people who adhere to different spiritual beliefs.

1. **During the next few days, take a personal inventory of your perceptions and attitudes in relationship to Muslims.**

    •   Which of your beliefs and attitudes would you say are the greatest hindrance to developing a heart-to-heart relationship in which you could share the good news about Jesus with a Muslim friend?

    •   In what ways have these beliefs and attitudes impacted your life and/or relationships with people around you?

    •   What do you consider to be the attitude or behavior that is most difficult for you to change?

2. **In keeping with Jesus' command to take the good news to *all* creation, what might you do to begin establishing relationships with Muslims? Which of the following options are you open to exploring?**

- Do you know any Muslims in your workplace, your school, or your community? (If you haven't already, perhaps it would be a good idea to introduce yourself!)

- Would you consider inviting a Muslim (or family) to join you at a community event or invite them into your home for a meal? If not, what do you think would be a good first get-together?

- If you don't know any Muslims, where is the nearest mosque or university? A mosque may host local community events, and groups for Muslim students may welcome your interest and hospitality.

HINTS FOR GROWING A MEANINGFUL RELATIONSHIP

As you seek to fulfill Jesus' command to "go into all the world and preach the good news," remember that there have been many centuries of division and fighting between the Big Three monotheisms — Judaism, Christianity, Islam. As a result, potential hot buttons and land mines are plentiful in any relationship you may have with a Muslim. So make an earnest decision not to be defensive, retaliatory, or presumptuous. Your relationship is about you, your friend, and Jesus — not about religious institutions or the history of hatred and shame.

MCJ

Understanding What Muslims Believe

If we truly wish to build a relationship with a Muslim friend, we need to explore areas of common interest. Christians and Muslims believe that there is only one God, which is a good place to start. But it is helpful if we understand more of what Muslims believe and are obligated to do. We must know enough to realize how sacred the Islamic faith is to Muslims so that we do not treat it with disregard. If we begin with the attitude that we are going to debunk "all of that Islamic stuff," we'll be done before we get a chance to introduce Jesus.

MCJ

LET'S THINK ABOUT IT

(4 minutes)

How easy is it to strike up an engaging, heart-to-heart conversation before we know anything about the person with whom we are speaking? (And remember, monologues about ourselves and our accomplishments don't count! They rarely engage the heart of the other person!)

If we want to have a significant, personal spiritual conversation with a Muslim — a conversation that steers clear of debate on political issues or pits Christianity against Islam — what might we need to know about what that person believes and values?

- For example, to what extent could you participate in a conversation about Muhammad's life? His motivation? The source of his teachings? What he taught about Jesus?
- To what extent could you talk with a Muslim friend about how important the foundational principles of Islam are to his or her daily life and hope for the future?
- To what extent could you participate in a conversation about what the Qur'an says about Jesus that might lead to a deeper conversation about him?

DVD OBSERVATIONS

As you watch the video segment for this session, use the following topics as a guide for taking notes.

The five pillars of Islam

    The Testimony (*Shahadah*)

    Prayer (*Salat*)

    The Fast (primarily during *Ramadan*)

    Giving (*Zakat*)

    Pilgrimage (*Hajj*)

Who was Muhammad?

What is the Qur'an?

Exploring spiritual truth with a Muslim

DVD DISCUSSION

1. Before you viewed the video, what did you know about the five pillars of Islam expressed in the Qur'an?

    What stood out to you as you learned about the five pillars that guide Muslims in the practice of their faith?

    How committed to their faith would you expect people who practiced these pillars to be?

2. How have you viewed Muhammad, and in what ways might the knowledge that — at least early in his life — Muhammad confronted polytheism and sought to turn people toward the one, true God influence your view?

- Born in Mecca in the late sixth century AD; his father had already died.
- Mother died when he was six years old; was raised by grand-father and uncle.
- First wife was prominent tradeswoman; he managed her cara-van, traveled widely, and discussed God with Christians, Jews, and polytheistic Arabs.
- By age forty he believed humankind was straying from God's path and diluting the truth.
- Reportedly God (or God's messenger, Gabriel the archangel — referred to as "the Holy Spirit" by Muslims today) gave him a series of divine messages.
- Was rejected when he publicly proclaimed these messages of obedience, judgment, and the primacy of one God — the God of Abraham — and called his countrymen to turn away from idolatry and return to the ways of Christians and Jews — "the people of the book."
- Persecuted, he and his believers moved to Yathrib (Medina) and Islam ("to surrender"; "to submit") began.
- Experienced many military successes that brought him great wealth; more tribes joined him.
- By 632 AD, when he died, Arabs were unified, had accepted his teachings and codified law, and Islam began spreading throughout North Africa, Syria, Iraq, Egypt, Persia (Iran), and even to Spain and France.

MCJ

3. How comfortable are you about reading the Qur'an in order to be conversant with Muslims about their spiritual views? What would you hope to gain from reading it?

How do you think a Muslim might respond if he or she knew that you voluntarily had read Islam's most holy book?

4. How do you respond to the idea that friendship is more important than theological debate when getting to know a Muslim?

How well do you listen without comment as another person shares his or her beliefs, respond when you do not know how to answer a question, or refrain from sharing your theological expertise when it might incite controversy?

When developing a relationship with a Muslim in which you can discuss spiritual matters, how might you find the right balance in steering clear of the more difficult questions and controversial issues without feeling that you are compromising the fundamentals of your faith?

5. What do you think is most challenging and most promising about seeking to love Muslim people as God loves them and sharing the good news of Jesus with them?

GROUP BIBLE EXPLORATION

(20 minutes)

Set Free to Love and Share Jesus

As recorded in John 8:31–32, Jesus said to those who believed him: "If you hold to my teaching, you are really my disciples. Then you will know the truth, and the truth will set you free." We often think of freedom in terms of being set free *from* something. But freedom also means being set free *to* something. For those of us who follow Jesus, the truth of Jesus sets us free *from* bondage to sin and sets us free *to* love people as God loves them.

1. Consider the three truths we explored during the previous session: (1) Jesus loves people and wants them to know him; (2) we have no need to fear because God promises to be with those who do his work; and (3) Jesus wants those whom he has set free to tell the good news to all people.

   a. To what extent might focusing on these truths set your heart free to love Muslims?

   b. How important is it for followers of Jesus — who want to be set free to love as he loves — to truly live by his teaching?

Muslims believe Islam's holy books to be God's truths and treat them with great reverence. These books include:

- The *Taureh* — what we call the Torah or Pentateuch;
- The *Zabur* — the Psalms of David, who is considered to be a prophet;
- The *Injil* — the Gospels — teachings of Jesus of Nazareth;
- The *Hadith* — although not technically an Islamic "holy book," a highly regarded collection of traditions and precedents set in place by Muhammad's life;
- The *Qur'an* — Islam's holiest book, believed to comprise the perfect and unimpeachable recordings of God's words that the angel Gabriel gave to Muhammad.

Muslim belief holds that the Qur'an has always existed in heaven in stone tablets (in Arabic) and that Gabriel helped Muhammad collect these revelations word-for-word from these tablets. Muhammad verbally transmitted these revelations, which are considered to be the final and complete revelation of God to humankind, but no complete written Qur'an existed at the time of his death in 632 AD. Different individuals wrote down the teachings and, by 652 AD, the "official" version of the Qur'an rendered all other versions obsolete.

Muslims believe the Qur'an is God speaking and do not associate it with any human authors. It is blasphemous to attribute the Qur'an even to Muhammad. To a Muslim, the Qur'an is a later revelation from God than the Bible; therefore, it is believed to be "more correct" than the Bible.

The Qur'an is organized into 114 *surahs* (titled chapters) by length — longest ones first. The verses are called *ayas* or *ayat*; the Arabic word *aya* is best translated "sign" or "miracle." Some *surahs* are poetic, others are stories, and some deal with life issues and practical aspects of religion. Interestingly, the Qur'an makes many references to Jesus (see Appendix). It says that Jesus — *Isa* — is the *word of God*, a spirit from God, and sits close to God.

By becoming familiar with the holy books of Islam, and particularly by reading the Qur'an, you will find more freedom in your relationship with your Muslim friends. Your sincerity in learning about *their* holy book will gain miles of respect and heart-felt gratitude for your openness.

MCJ

Exploring the Faith of Your Muslim Friend

Muslims are obliged to acknowledge certain *iman* — objects of doctrine — that are commonly confessed like this: "I believe in God, his angels, his books, his prophets, in the last day, and in God's predestined will." These fundamental statements of doctrine function in a way that is similar to the role of a church's statement of faith.

2. Examining Islam's six articles of faith will help us to better understand what our Muslim friends believe. By comparing Muslim beliefs to what the Bible teaches, we can identify similarities and differences and discover ways that Muslim beliefs can be a bridge to deeper friendships and more meaningful spiritual conversations. Consider each of the articles of faith summarized in the chart on pages 38–39, and then discuss the questions about pertinent biblical teaching and how these *iman* might lead to meaningful conversations.

Islam's articles of faith (*iman*) — to be confessed and believed*	How are these beliefs similar to/different from biblical teaching?	How might these beliefs build bridges to deeper spiritual conversations?
1. *There is one true, all-powerful, all-knowing God and none other.* Emphasis is on God's oneness and wholeness. God has no equal or division; thus the idea of the Trinity offends because it "lessens" God.		
2. *Angels are God's servants* who reveal his will, particularly to the prophets. Gabriel is the greatest angel.		
3. *Holy books are greatly revered* because they are representative of God and are his truths. Even the Arabic words are holy. The Qur'an is the holiest of books. As God's final and complete revelation it has precedence over the Bible because it came after the Bible.		

Islam's articles of faith (*iman*) — to be confessed and believed*	How are these beliefs similar to/different from biblical teaching?	How might these beliefs build bridges to deeper spiritual conversations?
4. *The prophets are men God used to speak his teaching and to guide men in righteous living.* The major prophets are Adam, Noah, Abraham, Moses, Jesus (called *Isa*, "his word," in the Qur'an; is the holiest and is sinless; virgin born), and Muhammad (the last and final prophet). Prophets cannot be denied, but they are not divine; they are role models.		
5. *The Day of Judgment is the greatly feared day when God weighs everyone's deeds and determines their eternal fate.* It is linked to the resurrection and follows wars, natural disasters, and the antichrist's appearance. Every person will either be saved or fall into hell.		
6. *Predestination.* Muslims understand fate to be predetermined by the supreme, all-powerful God whose will is final and absolute. God's will is not questioned.		

*For a more complete exploration of the *iman*, see *MCJ*, pp. 38–45.

Many people wrongly believe that Allah is the name of *a* god that Muslims worship. This is not the case. *Allah* is the Arabic word for *God*. Muhammad considered Islam to be a call to return to the one true God, the God of Abraham, whom he would naturally call *Allah*.

Allah is derived from the root *Al-llah*, which means "the god" or "the deity." The word is linguistically related to the Hebrew word *Elohim*. During Muhammad's time, Arab Christians used the word *Allah* for God. When a follower of Jesus today prays in Arabic, God is *Allah* and *Allah* is God. Every Arabic Bible also translates the word *God* as *Allah*. During his crucifixion, when Jesus cried out to the Father, he used the word *Alahi* (*Eli*) that is linguistically closer to the Arabic word translated as *God* than our modern use of the English word *God*.

MCJ

Finding Common Ground in Our Spiritual Disciplines

Many Muslims are committed, devout people who practice the five pillars of Islam. These spiritual disciplines include the Testimony, the Fast (primarily during Ramadan), Giving, Prayer, and the Hadj (pilgrimage to Mecca). Some of the spiritual disciplines that followers of Jesus practice are similar: we have a testimony of what we believe, we fast, we give, and we pray. Let's consider what some Bible passages say in relationship to these disciplines that will give us conversation points to explore with Muslims.

Our Testimony:

"Teacher, which is the greatest commandment in the Law?"

Jesus replied: "'Love the Lord your God with all your heart and with all your soul and with all your mind.' This is the first and greatest commandment. And the second is like it: 'Love your

neighbor as yourself.' All the Law and the Prophets hang on these
two commandments."

Matthew 22:36–40

3. Because Muslims consider Jesus to be a prophet of God, what agreement might you and a Muslim friend share if you were to talk about the Matthew teaching, what it means, and the importance of following it?

Fasting:

There, by the Ahava Canal, I proclaimed a fast, so that we might humble ourselves before our God and ask him for a safe journey for us and our children, with all our possessions. I was ashamed to ask the king for soldiers and horsemen to protect us from enemies on the road, because we had told the king, "The gracious hand of our God is on everyone who looks to him, but his great anger is against all who forsake him." So we fasted and petitioned our God about this, and he answered our prayer.

Ezra 8:21–23

Is this the kind of fast I have chosen, only a day for people to humble themselves? ... Is not this the kind of fasting I have chosen: to loose the chains of injustice and untie the cords of the yoke, to set the oppressed free and break every yoke? Is it not to share your food with the hungry and to provide the poor wanderer with shelter — when you see the naked, to clothe them, and not to turn away from your own flesh and blood?

Isaiah 58:5–7

Then Jesus was led by the Spirit into the wilderness to be tempted by the devil. After fasting forty days and forty nights, he was hungry. The tempter came to him and said, "If you are the Son of God, tell these stones to become bread."

Jesus answered, "It is written: 'Man shall not live on bread alone, but on every word that comes from the mouth of God.'"

Matthew 4:1 – 4

4. The Ramadan fast primarily commemorates the revelations God gave to Muhammad through the angel Gabriel. How might a Muslim friend respond to the idea of fasting in order to show humility before God and to focus attention on God's teaching and the work he wants his followers to do on earth?

What might you and a Muslim friend discover about your respective walks of faith if you were to talk about fasting and perhaps read the above passages together?

Giving:

There will always be poor people in the land. Therefore I command you to be openhanded toward your brothers and toward the poor and needy in your land.

Deuteronomy 15:11

It is a sin to despise one's neighbor, but blessed is the one who is kind to the needy.... Whoever oppresses the poor shows contempt for their Maker, but whoever is kind to the needy honors God.

Proverbs 14:21, 31

Whoever sows sparingly will also reap sparingly, and whoever sows generously will also reap generously. Each of you should give what you have decided in your heart to give, not reluctantly or under compulsion, for God loves a cheerful giver. And God is able to bless you abundantly, so that in all things at all times, having all that you need, you will abound in every good work.

2 Corinthians 9:6–8

5. To what extent might you and a Muslim friend share similar views about why you give and what types of giving please God?

Might you and your Muslim friend choose to give in response to the same needs, and perhaps give together such as by working side-by-side in a food pantry or other charity? Why or why not?

Prayer:

Then I acknowledged my sin to you and did not cover up my iniquity. I said, "I will confess my transgressions to the Lord." And you forgave the guilt of my sin. Therefore let all the faithful pray to you while you may be found; surely the rising of the mighty waters will not reach them.

Psalm 32:5–6

One of those days Jesus went out to a mountainside to pray, and spent the night praying to God.

Luke 6:12

Rejoice always, pray continually, give thanks in all circumstances; for this is God's will for you in Christ Jesus.

1 Thessalonians 5:16–18

6. Prayer is a daily requirement for Muslims. Because the prayer life of a follower of Jesus is often more private than public, your Muslim friend may not realize that prayer is important to you. How might the above verses help you to share why you pray and provide an opportunity for both you and your Muslim friend to talk about your relationship and communication with God?

7. How do you think your relationship with a Muslim friend might deepen if you talked together about these spiritual disciplines?

Do you see any risk in sharing together at this level? Explain your answer.

PERSONAL REFLECTION

(3 minutes)

Fouad Elias Accad writes in his book *Building Bridges: Christianity and Islam* (NavPress, 1997): "Suppose a man who had shaved off all his hair and who wrapped himself in a bright orange sarong came into my community proclaiming 'God's Truth.' No matter how sincere and loving he was, I would be dead set against renouncing my culture to accept his 'truth' about God and becoming like him. But, if he had behaved according to the ways of my culture, and treated my beliefs with respect, it would be far easier to hear what he was saying and to seriously consider it."

In what way(s) do you understand this quotation better as a result of what you have explored and discussed during this session?

What are your thoughts and feelings as you learn more about the beliefs and practices of Muslims?

What new ideas have you gained for engaging in personal, spiritual conversations with Muslims?

- *Regarding the fast, don't eat in front of your Muslim friend during Ramadan.*
- *Regarding prayer, be careful not to walk in front of a praying Muslim.* Because Muslims don't see Christians praying as they do, they may think that you don't pray. Feel free to let them know that you pray, and if you pray with them, stand or kneel, holding your hands with the palms upward.
- *Regarding giving, be quick to notice what is virtuous and participate as you can.* Humbly share with your Muslim friend your own giving practices and motivation for doing so.
- *Recognize that Jesus has said something relevant regarding every Muslim practice.* Because the teachings of Jesus are important to your Muslim friend, you will have all the conversational material you need for deepening your relationship.

MCJ

CLOSING

(1 minute)

Pray about what you have discovered during today's session and how you might apply what you have learned about Islam to your life and your relationships with Muslims. Pray that God will prepare you with a loving, open, and respectful heart for the people he desires you to befriend. Ask God to deliver you from fears and feelings of inadequacy that would hinder you from obeying Jesus' command to go and preach the good news.

STEPS TO TAKE ON YOUR OWN

Imagine what might happen if we as individuals—and the church as a whole—became more diligent about living out our walk with God and sharing the gospel message with people who do not know him. What if we became more intentional and faithful in prayer because we love to communicate with God? What if we devoted ourselves to fasting in preparation to do his work in the world? What if we held God's Word in great esteem and committed ourselves to obeying it with all our heart, soul, and mind? What if we demonstrated our love for God and our neighbor by being more generous in giving to those who are in need?

1. **Consider the spiritual disciplines discussed in this session.**

   • What transforming work would you expect God to accomplish in your heart and life if you were to pursue these disciplines more diligently?

   • In what ways might your example lead people around you to view followers of Jesus in a different, more positive light?

2. **God desires you to share the good news of Jesus with people who do not know him. Set aside some uninterrupted time to evaluate your commitment to God and to obeying his Word. Then write out your commitment.**

   Starting today, I will begin to take the following steps because I desire to know God better and to share the good news of Jesus with Muslims and people of other faiths whom he loves ...

3. In addition to reading parts of the Qur'an in order to better understand the spiritual practices of Muslims and to talk knowledgably with them about their faith, it is essential that you know what the Bible says about these subjects. Consider the topics below and choose the top two or three that you will study in greater depth.

- Prayer

- Fasting

- Giving

- The one true God

- Angels

- The prophets, particularly Jesus — his life and teachings

HINTS FOR RELATIONSHIP-BUILDING CONVERSATIONS WITH MUSLIMS

- Express sincere interest in your friend and in what he or she thinks about God.
- Avoid me-versus-you debates.
- Don't insult Muhammad.
- To show proper respect, refer to Jesus as "the Christ" or "the Messiah."
- Never view your conversation or relationship as simply a way to "win a convert."

Jesus: The Bridge to Muslims

The message we carry is Jesus. Not church, not capitalism, not democracy, not doctrine, not the religion of Christianity, not Calvin or Luther. If we truly wish to be able to build a relationship with a Muslim friend, the most important thing we can do is to follow Jesus' lead. Jesus himself is the good news.

MCJ

LET'S THINK ABOUT IT

Perhaps the most important question ever asked was Jesus' question to Peter: "Who do you say I am?" When Peter replied by saying, "Christ, the Son of the living God," Jesus said he was blessed because that knowledge had been revealed to him by God in heaven (Matthew 16:15–17).

- Do you believe that Jesus still asks people to answer this question — to decide who he is? Why or why not?
- What role do you think those of us who follow Jesus have in preparing people to answer this question in the way Peter did?
- What are some of the methods we use to do this, and how effective are they?

DVD OBSERVATIONS

As you watch the video segment for this session, use the following topics as a guide for taking notes.

Muslim perceptions of Christianity

What Muslims believe about Jesus

Jesus is the message we preach

Share the stories of Jesus

DVD DISCUSSION

8 minutes*(8 minutes)*

1. If you are a follower of Jesus, how did it feel to realize that most Muslims identify "Christians" with a religious/political system and what they see in the media, including gang violence, Hollywood morality, and disintegrating families?

    In what ways might this perception on the part of Muslims be similar to the perception of people in the West that all followers of Islam want to kill people who are not Muslims? How do you think a Muslim might feel about this identification?

    Why, then, is it important for us to distinguish between being a *Christian* and being a *follower of Jesus* as we seek to build sincere, meaningful relationships with Muslims?

2. It can be unsettling when those of us who may be used to presenting Christianity in terms of a doctrinal system must change our approach to a more personal, active sharing of who Jesus is and how we have experienced him. What challenges do we face in adjusting our focus, choosing topics to share, and even letting go of the language we typically use as we try to do this?

   How might the apostle Paul's strategy to "know nothing ... except Jesus" help us in our efforts?

3. In what ways does the knowledge that many Muslims are "pro-Jesus" open up new ways to talk with them about Jesus?

4. Christians sometimes take offense to the Muslim belief that Jesus is a prophet because they feel it belittles Jesus, but what does being a prophet mean to a Muslim?

5. Which stories that Jesus told and which stories about his life do you think best communicate who he is to Muslims? Why?

    Which of these stories do you feel you can tell well, and with which ones might you need to become more familiar?

GROUP BIBLE EXPLORATION

Know Nothing but Jesus

Although Muslims often respond negatively to the words *Christian* and *Christianity* because these words are weighted with hidden meanings and historical grievances, they often respond positively to Jesus Christ. So rather than arguing the disparities of the two faiths or trying to convince a Muslim to believe a checklist of Christian practices or theology, it's more helpful to begin by showing our Muslim friends how they can believe in God more fully through Jesus Christ.

1. When Jesus is our focus, we can enjoy some "shared ground" from which we can patiently move toward deeper discussions of doctrine as the Holy Spirit leads and our Muslim friend desires. Notice how the apostle Paul approached his ministry to the Corinthians:

    > When I came to you, I did not come with eloquence or human wisdom as I proclaimed to you the testimony about God. For I resolved to know nothing while I was with you except Jesus Christ and him crucified. I came to you in weakness with great fear and trembling. My message and my preaching were not with wise and persuasive words, but with a demonstration of the Spirit's power, so that your faith might not rest on human wisdom, but on God's power.
    >
    > 1 Corinthians 2:1–5

    a. In what ways does Paul's explanation of his ministry to the Corinthians describe the situation that we, as followers of Jesus, face when we seek to share the good news with Muslims?

SESSION 3—Jesus: The Bridge to Muslims | 55

b. If you have attempted to tell people about Jesus through eloquence, human wisdom, or persuasive words, what was the result, and would you try that approach again? Why or why not?

THE KEY TO ESTABLISHING COMMUNICATION

> If you earnestly wish to open communication with your Muslim friends, you have to be sacrificial about it. Some of the most important words and phrases in your faith will have to be put on a shelf for a while. As Paul did, you have to be willing to be all things to all people, even to become like those who are under a law, in order that you might gain some.
>
> *MCJ*

Practice Telling Jesus Stories

Although many of us in the West are tempted to use logic and even debate to try to "prove" the validity of Christianity, faith in Jesus comes by seeing him, being touched by him, and being led by his Spirit — not through intellectual argument. Jesus stories help us to share who Jesus is in a way that touches the hearts of people who do not know him, especially Muslims.

In general, Muslims are naturally drawn toward Jesus. They consider him to be the holiest prophet in Islam. And even today, Muslims who live in the Middle East experience life through a culture that is closer to the culture of Jesus' day than to what we experience in the West. Although their understanding of him and his work is not the same as ours, most Muslims are quite willing to explore what the Bible says about what Jesus did and said. So let's consider three Jesus stories and talk about what a Muslim might discover about Jesus through each story.

2. Read Matthew 15:29–38:

> Jesus left there and went along the Sea of Galilee. Then he
> went up on a mountainside and sat down. Great crowds came
> to him, bringing the lame, the blind, the crippled, the mute
> and many others, and laid them at his feet; and he healed them.
> The people were amazed when they saw the mute speaking,
> the crippled made well, the lame walking and the blind seeing.
> And they praised the God of Israel.
>
> Jesus called his disciples to him and said, "I have compas-
> sion for these people; they have already been with me three
> days and have nothing to eat. I do not want to send them away
> hungry, or they may collapse on the way."
>
> His disciples answered, "Where could we get enough
> bread in this remote place to feed such a crowd?"
>
> "How many loaves do you have?" Jesus asked.
>
> "Seven," they replied, "and a few small fish."
>
> He told the crowd to sit down on the ground. Then he
> took the seven loaves and the fish, and when he had given
> thanks, he broke them and gave them to the disciples, and they
> in turn to the people. They all ate and were satisfied. After-
> ward the disciples picked up seven basketfuls of broken pieces
> that were left over. The number of those who ate was four
> thousand men, besides women and children.

a. How might this picture of the crowds who followed Jesus, his
    miracles of healing and feeding, and his compassionate heart
    lead a Muslim to want to know more about Jesus?

b.   How might you begin a conversation with a Muslim friend about how Jesus desires to demonstrate his love and compassion to people today?

3.   Read Matthew 22:23 – 33:

> That same day the Sadducees, who say there is no resurrection, came to him with a question. "Teacher," they said, "Moses told us that if a man dies without having children, his brother must marry the widow and raise up offspring for him. Now there were seven brothers among us. The first one married and died, and since he had no children, he left his wife to his brother. The same thing happened to the second and third brother, right on down to the seventh. Finally, the woman died. Now then, at the resurrection, whose wife will she be of the seven, since all of them were married to her?"
>
> Jesus replied, "You are in error because you do not know the Scriptures or the power of God. At the resurrection people will neither marry nor be given in marriage; they will be like the angels in heaven. But about the resurrection of the dead — have you not read what God said to you, 'I am the God of Abraham, the God of Isaac, and the God of Jacob'? He is not the God of the dead but of the living."
>
> When the crowds heard this, they were astonished at his teaching.

a.   Muslims have great respect for prophets — for those who speak the truth about God. What might they discover about the wisdom and truth of Jesus' words from this story?

b.   What other aspects of this story might capture the attention of a Muslim?

4.   Read Luke 7:36–47:

> When one of the Pharisees invited Jesus to have dinner with him, he went to the Pharisee's house and reclined at the table. A woman in that town who lived a sinful life learned that Jesus was eating at the Pharisee's house, so she came there with an alabaster jar of perfume. As she stood behind him at his feet weeping, she began to wet his feet with her tears. Then she wiped them with her hair, kissed them and poured perfume on them.
>
> When the Pharisee who had invited him saw this, he said to himself, "If this man were a prophet, he would know who is touching him and what kind of woman she is — that she is a sinner."
>
> Jesus answered him, "Simon, I have something to tell you."
>
> "Tell me, teacher," he said.
>
> "Two people owed money to a certain moneylender. One owed him five hundred denarii, and the other fifty. Neither of them had the money to pay him back, so he forgave the debts of both. Now which of them will love him more?"
>
> Simon replied, "I suppose the one who had the bigger debt forgiven."
>
> "You have judged correctly," Jesus said.
>
> Then he turned toward the woman and said to Simon, "Do you see this woman? I came into your house. You did not give me any water for my feet, but she wet my feet with her tears and wiped them with her hair. You did not give me a kiss, but this woman, from the time I entered, has not stopped kissing my feet. You did not put oil on my head, but she has poured

perfume on my feet. Therefore, I tell you, her many sins have been forgiven — as her great love has shown. But whoever has been forgiven little loves little."

a. What insights into Jesus' wisdom, heart, and character are evident in this story, and what might they mean to a Muslim?

b. What does this story reveal about how important our character and heart attitudes are to Jesus, and what kind of conversation might we have about how Jesus sees the difference between religion and true faith?

c. What might we discover through this story about how to live and love others as Jesus loves, and why might this be meaningful to a Muslim?

True Faith Is to Know and to Follow

A deep and thorough understanding of the Scriptures is vital if we are to effectively point our friends to a complete understanding of who Jesus is and why he came. But we must always be careful not to let our understanding of doctrine take the place of a living relationship with Jesus Christ. The path to genuine friendships with Muslims begins when they recognize us as people who seek to follow the ways of God and be more like Jesus.

5. In this, as in everything, Jesus is our example. Notice how he responded (Matthew 23:13 – 28) toward religious leaders of his day who emphasized adherence to the rules of religion but lacked the justice, mercy, righteousness, and compassion of true faith:

> Woe to you, teachers of the law and Pharisees, you hypocrites! You shut the door of the kingdom of heaven in people's faces.... You give a tenth of your spices — mint, dill and cumin. But you have neglected the more important matters of the law — justice, mercy and faithfulness. You should have practiced the latter, without neglecting the former. You blind guides! You strain out a gnat but swallow a camel.... You clean the outside of the cup and dish, but inside they are full of greed and self-indulgence.... You are like whitewashed tombs, which look beautiful on the outside but on the inside are full of the bones of the dead and everything unclean. In the same way, on the outside you appear to people as righteous but on the inside you are full of hypocrisy and wickedness.

a. Might Jesus accuse his followers today of shutting Muslims out of the kingdom of heaven? Why or why not?

b. If we truly have a living relationship with Jesus, what do you think a Muslim might expect to see exhibited in our lives and through our relationships with them?

PERSONAL REFLECTION

I (Carl) was sitting in a hotel lobby in a small, southern Iraqi town, rubbing my eyes after a short nap, when three young staff members walked over from the front desk and sat down. They were curious about me and my friends, who had left me there to rest. "What are you doing in Iraq?" asked one of the guys. "Aren't you Americans? My friend says you are Christians."

"Yes, most of us are Americans," I answered, "but we live here in the Middle East. What do you mean ... you think we might be Christian?"

"You know," he said, "Christians! People who believe in Israel and the Trinity, and don't like us." He said this without hesitation, and unfortunately, it is a common opinion.

I had already learned not to defend all of Christendom — the good or the bad — so I said, "Well, I can't speak for others, but I'd love to tell you who we really are." They were hooked (and obviously bored in their jobs) and pulled an overstuffed sofa closer to hear my story.

"We are people of faith. Like you. People who believe in the one true God. Like you. People who want to love their wives and children and do good. Like you. We take prayer seriously. We want to be godly and act justly. Like you."

I continued: "We also try to follow the ways, teachings, and life of Jesus the Messiah. He's our model for all we do and think and say. We're not very good at it, but this is our goal."

When someone asks if you are a Christian, what are the first words that usually come out of your mouth?

Which opportunities and barriers might your response establish for future conversations, particularly with Muslims?

What might you gain if you respond with a question such as, "What do you mean by *Christian?*"

CLOSING

(1 minute)

Pray about what you have discovered during today's session and how you might apply these discoveries to your life and relationships with Muslims. Ask God to continue his work in your heart and mind — focusing every thought, action, and conversation on Jesus and Jesus alone. Ask him to guide you to Muslim people who are eager to hear the story of Jesus so that they may discover what it means to have a personal relationship with him.

WE PREACH JESUS THE CHRIST

To open dialogue, what I find most effective and most Christlike is to stay focused on Jesus. I talk about his leadership style, his wisdom, his teachings, and his miracles. I have sat and prayed with many influential Muslim businessmen and political leaders, and never once have I been chastised for talking about *Isa al-Messiah*: Jesus the Christ.

MCJ

STEPS TO TAKE ON YOUR OWN

Despite theological differences between Christianity and Islam, there is a gold mine running throughout the Qur'an: his name is Jesus (*Isa*). The Qur'an mentions Jesus almost one hundred times, all with great reverence. It is perhaps the greatest inroad we have to reach the hearts of our Muslim friends.

The appendix of this book (beginning on page 87) provides an overview of what the Qur'an says about Jesus Christ — his life, character, death, relationship to God — and his followers. For each reference in the Qur'an, the appendix also provides a corresponding reference in the Bible. Choose one or more of the topics and with a copy of the Qur'an and your Bible, begin to study the similarities and differences between Jesus in the Qur'an and Jesus in the Bible. This will be a great help to you in talking about Jesus with a Muslim friend.

HINTS FOR SHARING JESUS WITH MUSLIMS

- Never attack the person of Muhammad or the Qur'an.
- Guard against being defensive about God and his Word; deflect verbal attacks gently and patiently.
- Steer away from political arguments; avoid a confrontational, apologetic approach; no matter what, don't argue.
- Don't assume that you know what a Muslim believes; ask questions.
- Be a great listener!
- Talk about Jesus with respect; use his name with a title such as Jesus the Christ or Jesus the Messiah.
- Try to avoid using terms that are red flags for Muslims, including *Son of God*, *Christian*, and *church*.
- Make a clear distinction between the "Christian" West with its image of bad morals, lack of spirituality, etc. and what a true follower of Jesus is like.

- Don't have the attitude that you know all truth; instead, communicate that you know the One who is the Truth and that you continue to grow in your understanding of him as you follow him.
- Share the good news when appropriate, but don't try to "convert," "fix," or push your Muslim friend to think about Jesus the way you do.
- Be yourself — multidimensional, full of integrity and love, natural, encouraging — and talk about things that matter most in your life and in the life of your Muslim friend.
- Be involved in Muslims' lives — get to know their children, invite them to your home, and be available when they call you.
- Share about Jesus and your personal experience with him not because you feel obligated to but because you love him and you care enough about your Muslim friend that you want your friend to know who Jesus is and what he has done.
- Feel free to ask if you may pray aloud for your Muslim friends; they are people of prayer. Pray for God's Spirit to touch them and for blessing on their family, work, and home.

Building Bridges through Relationship

Often people ask me how I got such a love for Muslims. My typical answer is, "I don't love Muslims. I love people like Samir, Ahmad, Ali, and their families. They just happen to be Muslims." It's a funny idea that we can love a group of people or an ideology or a principle. It seems to me that Jesus loves individual people.

MCJ

LET'S THINK ABOUT IT

(4 minutes)

When we see people who are quite different from us — maybe they dress differently, speak a different language, listen to weird music, cook odd-smelling food, or in some other way simply don't fit in with how we live — we tend to respond negatively.

- In what way do our responses help or hinder us in fulfilling Jesus' command to preach the good news about him to *all* people?
- If we sincerely desire to reach out to people whom we view as "outsiders" and to love them as Jesus loves them, what might our first steps toward a one-on-one relationship look like?

DVD OBSERVATIONS

(20 minutes)

As you watch the video segment for this session, use the following topics as a guide for taking notes.

How Jesus interacted with people who are on the "outside"

Full of grace

Full of truth

Establishing relationships with Muslims

Reach out with hospitality

Offer to pray

Be bold in going to where they are

Be encouraged by Jesus

DVD DISCUSSION

(10 minutes)

1. Consider how Jesus responded to the Samaritan woman (discussed in session one of this series), sinners, lepers, prostitutes, tax collectors, and others who were not highly regarded by God-fearing Jews of his day. What do you learn from his manner of relating to those "outsiders" that can help us befriend Muslims and love them as Jesus loves them?

   What may keep us from responding as Jesus would to Muslims and other people whom we consider to be "outsiders"?

   Which sincere attitudes of the heart and specific practices might we need to cultivate in order to reach out to "outsiders" with the love of Jesus?

2. We have learned that not all truth is helpful when beginning a relationship with a Muslim — insisting on certain truths can shut down a relationship before it really begins. But as a relationship progresses and respect and trust in the other person's spiritual integrity grows,

70 | MUSLIMS, CHRISTIANS, AND JESUS Participant's Guide

how might you know when it is time to introduce some of the more difficult truths about Jesus?

3. How do you feel about praying for and with a Muslim even early in your relationship before you know much about your shared spiritual interests?

4. Think back to the attitudes you had toward Islam and Muslims before the start of this series. In what ways do you view Muslims differently now, and why?

5. Reconsider Jesus' command to preach the good news to *all* people. How willing and equipped are you to fulfill this command in relationship to Muslims? What further equipping do you need, and how will you attain it?

6. What might we, as a group that has grown through this video study, do to learn more about Muslims who live near us and to take steps to meet them?

JESUS' KIND OF PEOPLE

Jesus seems to have had a favorable bias toward the "wrong crowd." I hate to say it, but Muslims probably fit into this category! They're outsiders here in the West: wrong religion, wrong language, wrong dress and customs. Sounds like Jesus' kind of people.

MCJ

GROUP BIBLE EXPLORATION

Showing Hospitality

If someone told you that a key way to reach out in friendship to a Muslim neighbor or coworker is to *party*, you might be surprised, but it's true. Hospitality, expressed by opening your home to guests in order to share meals and conversation, often is an effective way to break down barriers and initiate meaningful relationships between you and Muslims.

1. Hospitality is highly valued among Muslims. The gracious hospitality Abraham showed to three travelers is similar to how Muslims living in the Middle East today reach out to others:

    > The LORD appeared to Abraham near the great trees of Mamre while he was sitting at the entrance to his tent in the heat of the day. Abraham looked up and saw three men standing nearby. When he saw them, he hurried from the entrance of his tent to meet them and bowed low to the ground.
    >
    > He said, "If I have found favor in your eyes, my lord, do not pass your servant by. Let a little water be brought, and then you may all wash your feet and rest under this tree. Let me get you something to eat, so you can be refreshed and then go on your way — now that you have come to your servant."
    >
    > "Very well," they answered, "do as you say."
    >
    > So Abraham hurried into the tent to Sarah. "Quick," he said, "get three seahs of the finest flour and knead it and bake some bread."
    >
    > Then he ran to the herd and selected a choice, tender calf and gave it to a servant, who hurried to prepare it. He then brought some curds and milk and the calf that had been prepared, and set these before them. While they ate, he stood near them under a tree.
    >
    > Genesis 18:1 – 8

a. What does this story reveal about Abraham's heart and his desire to truly meet the needs of his visitors?

b. In what ways do you think the social environment that Abraham created would encourage warm, friendly conversation and provide an opportunity to begin a meaningful relationship?

2. Jesus taught his disciples with these words:

> You are the light of the world. A town built on a hill cannot be hidden. Neither do people light a lamp and put it under a bowl. Instead they put it on its stand, and it gives light to everyone in the house. In the same way, let your light shine before others, that they may see your good deeds and glorify your Father in heaven.
>
> Matthew 5:14–16

a. Considering how infrequently many Americans open their homes to people they do not know well, how important do you think extending hospitality to Muslims is to being a light in the world?

b. Which heart attitudes are necessary, and how might we express them, if we want our hospitality to bring praise to God rather than to ourselves?

3. Many Muslims who live in the West have never been invited into an American's home. How would you feel if you were a Muslim living in a "Christian" country ... and no one invited you to a home for even a meal?

How does that make you, as a follower of Jesus, feel and what are you willing to do about it?

- It is not hard to meet Muslims. Start out by saying something easy like, "Hi, how are you?" Then move to things like, "Where do you or your family originally come from?"

- Women should dress modestly around Muslims and should not offer to shake a Muslim man's hand unless he first offers his hand.

- Never use your left hand to shake hands or to eat with. Do not show the bottom of your feet.

- Great food — and lots of it — is a plus to winning Muslims' trust and their hearts. Cook twice as much as you think you need.

- Remember that pork, alcohol, and dogs are viewed as "dirty" by Muslims and must be avoided.

- In Eastern cultures, it's polite to say *no* several times to an offer, so instead of asking what beverages they would like, present choices of fruit juice, soda, coffee, and tea.

- As a meal begins, say something like, "Our family has a tradition to honor God by saying thank you for this food and for you. Do you mind if we do that?" Then pray naturally, conversationally. Don't be surprised when Muslims keep their heads up and eyes open when they pray.

MCJ

Showing Grace to Outsiders

Jesus seems always to have sought out the "wrong" people, the down-and-out sinners who needed his mercy, in order to lead them out of where they were and into a new place. He looked for and saw the lepers, the blind, the beggars, and the women when no one else did. He saw the seeker before the seeker saw him.

4. As you read the following passages of Scripture, notice what Jesus saw and how he met people at their point of need.

> When Jesus came down from the mountainside, large crowds followed him. A man with leprosy came and knelt before him and said, "Lord, if you are willing, you can make me clean."
>
> Jesus reached out his hand and touched the man. "I am willing," he said. "Be clean!" Immediately he was cleansed of his leprosy. Then Jesus said to him, "See that you don't tell anyone. But go, show yourself to the priest and offer the gift Moses commanded, as a testimony to them."
>
> Matthew 8:1 – 4

> Then they came to Jericho. As Jesus and his disciples, together with a large crowd, were leaving the city, a blind man, Bartimaeus (which means "son of Timaeus"), was sitting by the roadside begging. When he heard that it was Jesus of Nazareth, he began to shout, "Jesus, Son of David, have mercy on me!"
>
> Many rebuked him and told him to be quiet, but he shouted all the more, "Son of David, have mercy on me!"
>
> Jesus stopped and said, "Call him."
>
> So they called to the blind man, "Cheer up! On your feet! He's calling you." Throwing his cloak aside, he jumped to his feet and came to Jesus.
>
> "What do you want me to do for you?" Jesus asked him.
>
> The blind man said, "Rabbi, I want to see."
>
> "Go," said Jesus, "your faith has healed you." Immediately he received his sight and followed Jesus along the road.
>
> Mark 10:46 – 52

> As he approached the town gate, a dead person was being carried out — the only son of his mother, and she was a widow. And a large crowd from the town was with her. When the Lord saw her, his heart went out to her and he said, "Don't cry."
>
> Then he went up and touched the bier they were carrying him on, and the bearers stood still. He said, "Young man, I say

to you, get up!" The dead man sat up and began to talk, and Jesus gave him back to his mother.

Luke 7:12 – 15

a. What do our Muslim neighbors need us to see in them? That they are lonely? That they feel misunderstood and afraid? That they, too, are created in God's image?

b. How can we, as followers of Jesus, keep our focus on the needs of the other person and guard against self-serving agendas creeping into our relationships?

It's about the Person, not Religion

I (Carl) have found that when I feel the need to defend Christianity I dig myself a deep hole that is hard to escape.... Religions fight each other. They bicker and compete and try to win the other into their own. But we don't do that. We just lift up Jesus. We follow him, love him, and serve him. We present him as the good news.

5. When we engage in earnest spiritual conversations with our Muslim friends, it is easy for us to slip into the familiar mind-set of our own religious traditions. We tend to forget that the message we share is about Jesus, not the religion known as Christianity. It's an issue that

followers of Jesus have struggled with since the days of the apostles. Peter's recognition that God accepted Gentiles because of their faith in Jesus is most helpful:

> Then Peter began to speak: "I now realize how true it is that God does not show favoritism but accepts from every nation the one who fears him and does what is right. You know the message God sent to the people of Israel, announcing the good news of peace through Jesus Christ, who is Lord of all.... He commanded us to preach to the people and to testify that he is the one whom God appointed as judge of the living and the dead. All the prophets testify about him that everyone who believes in him receives forgiveness of sins through his name."
>
> While Peter was still speaking these words, the Holy Spirit came on all who heard the message. The circumcised believers who had come with Peter were astonished that the gift of the Holy Spirit had been poured out even on Gentiles.
>
> Acts 10:34–36, 42–45

a. Consider how you think this passage applies to Muslims who come to know Jesus as their Savior and submit to his teachings. To what extent is it viable for Muslims (which in Arabic means "submitted to God") to maintain their cultural identity while aligning themselves as followers of Jesus who obey his spiritual and moral teachings?

b. Culturally, Muslims and Christians today live in different worlds. How might the way a Muslim lives out a personal relationship with Jesus within the context of his or her own culture differ from the way a Western Christian might live? Might we each, like the early Jewish believers, be astonished that God has poured out his Spirit on them even as on us?

HINTS FOR FOCUSING ON THE PERSON, NOT THE RELIGION

To turn your focus away from being religious:

- *Don't be defensive.* You have nothing to defend. God doesn't need help with his reputation, and the Bible can stand on its own. The defensive one is usually the one who is standing on shaky ground. Religious people are defensive.
- *Don't argue.* Just don't. The next time someone says something you don't like or you don't agree with, try not arguing. See what happens. Religious people love arguments.
- *Don't carry yourself as if you know all truth.* We know the One who is the Truth and, as we grow closer to him, we understand more. But how much of Jesus do we really know? Religious people always claim to know more.

MCJ

PERSONAL REFLECTION

(2 minutes)

The whole message of God can be summarized in one brief sentence: Love God and love people. Numerous times the Bible says to "love your neighbor." And it's clear from the teachings of Jesus that our "neighbor" is basically anyone we meet who is in need (which would be everyone because all of us need Jesus).

Reflect on what you have learned about loving God and loving people during this study. To what extent do you feel that you can love Muslims as Jesus loves them?

HINTS FOR EXPLORING WHAT THE BIBLE SAYS ABOUT JESUS

- Through natural, sincere conversation let people know that you are a person of faith who enjoys learning more about Jesus.
- Invite Muslims to *discuss* Jesus, who is an interesting and controversial figure of history, *not to attend a Bible study*. Invite other neighbors, and meet with whoever responds, even if it's only one couple.
- Never write in the Qur'an or Bible or place it on the floor or the ground. Muslims consider this to be highly disrespectful.
- Focus your study on Jesus. You might read all the passages about him in the Qur'an and read the gospel of Luke. At least initially focus on areas of agreement and allow the Holy Spirit to do his work.

MCJ

CLOSING

Ask God to guide you to Muslims who are hungry to experience Jesus' love, truth, and grace. Pray for an open heart that will love Muslims sincerely. Pray for hands and feet that will labor sacrificially to care for the needs of Muslims like the Good Samaritan did for the injured man. Ask God to help you become more like Jesus as you follow in his steps and share his good news with Muslims.

STEPS TO TAKE ON YOUR OWN

Since the events of September 11, 2001, a thirst has awakened. I (Carl) have seen among followers of Jesus a desire to become more familiar with this religion called Islam. My heart surges with hope as I see followers of Jesus choose the road less traveled, driven to learn and see if there is a way to reach out to Muslims.

It is an exciting moment to not only realize that you have opportunities to befriend Muslims but to know in your heart that God desires for you—wherever you live, or whatever your circumstances—to share the good news of Jesus with them.

While the truths of these sessions are fresh in your mind, seek God's wisdom in setting a course for meeting and befriending Muslims. Write out:

- My heart for loving God and loving Muslims:

- My goals for establishing meaningful relationships with Muslims:

- What I hope to share with Muslims I meet:

- How I hope to grow in love, grace, and truth through my experiences:

HINTS FOR RESPECTING MUSLIM WOMEN

In the eyes of Westerners, one of Islam's glaring flaws is its medieval perspectives on women's rights. This should not surprise us because the model for Islamic law is about twelve centuries old. Although many Arab/Muslim nations are moving to change this perspective on women, other fundamentalist Muslim countries continue to structure their governments according to *Sharia* — Islamic law.

The strongest elements of Islamic law came about when women were not considered to be equal to men. So in Islamic states today, a woman's legal valuation is about half that of a man in court cases, for inheritance, and for compensation. A woman is assumed to be of her husband's religion, so if a Muslim man marries a Christian woman, she is a Muslim. Muslim men can marry Christian or Jewish women, but Muslim women cannot marry outside their faith.

Issues for Muslim women vary according to their particular families and the version of Islam they practice. For the most part, Muslim women in fundamentalist Muslim countries are to be in the home — not doing outside jobs and attending school. In other Muslim nations, women are not *required* to stay home — but it often happens. Muslim women in the West often (but certainly not always) come from more open-minded families. So they may not wear a traditional head covering and accompanying veil (*abaya* or *hijab*). They may also hold professional jobs.

In general, Muslim women are to repress their sexuality and dress modestly as the Qur'an dictates. They are "protected" from impurity and dishonor by staying near home and being under the watchful eyes of male relatives when they are away from home. Because Muslims honor purity, it is best if women befriend women and men befriend men — particularly if you are meeting in a home or alone.

The homebound status of Muslim women can make them hungry for friendship. A Western woman can start to build a relationship with a Muslim woman by talking with her about her life, her heart, her experiences, and her beliefs. These early conversations will often reveal the Muslim woman's interest in the deeper things of faith.

MCJ

APPENDIX

What the Qur'an* Says about Jesus

The Conception and Birth of Jesus

- God foreordained the birth of Jesus (*Isa*) — Q 3:47; Q 19:20–22 (Luke 1:34–35)
- God commanded Jesus' birth — Q 3:47 (Luke 1:31, 35)
- Jesus' birth was a sign to mankind — Q 21:91 (Luke 2:8–20; Matthew 2:1–12)
- The day of Jesus' birth was blessed — Q 19:33 (Luke 2:10–14)
- Jesus is the son of Mary (*Maryam*) — Q 3:45 (Matthew 13:55)
- No man had touched Mary when she became pregnant with Jesus — Q 19:20; Q 21:91; Q 3:47; Q 66:12 (Matthew 1:18)
- God sent his Spirit to Mary and it took the form of a man — Q 21:91; Q 66:12 (Luke 1:26–35)
- God gave Mary a sinless son — Q 19:19 (Luke 1:35)

---

* (with corresponding references from the Bible)

The Character of Jesus

- God made Jesus an example to the people of Israel — Q 43:59 (Isaiah 49:6)
- God commanded Jesus to honor his mother — Q 19:32 (John 19:26)
- God did not make Jesus proud or rebellious — Q 19:32 (Luke 2:51–52)
- Jesus is righteous — Q 3:46; Q 6:85 (John 8:46)
- Jesus only did what God told him to do — Q 5:117 (John 5:19, 30)

The Death of Jesus

- People plotted against Jesus — Q 3:54–56 (Acts 2:23; Matthew 12:14)
- God can do anything he wants to — even allow Jesus to die — Q 5:17, 117 (Luke 1:37)
- God said to Jesus that he would make him die — Q 3:55 (Mark 14:36; Isaiah 53:10)
- When God made Christ die, God himself became the over-seer — Q 5:117 (Isaiah 53:4, 8, 10)
- The ones who killed Christ weren't really the killers, because it was God's plan — Q 3:54–56 (Acts 2:23)
- Christ was dead and God raised him — Q 19:33 (Acts 2:23–24)
- The day Jesus died was blessed — Q 19:33 (Isaiah 53:10–12)

Jesus Being Exalted

- The knowledge of the last days is God's — Q 41:47; Q 43:61 (Matthew 24:36)
- God aided Jesus with the Holy Spirit — Q 2:87; Q 2:253; Q 5:110 (Matthew 3:16; Luke 4:18; Acts 10:38)
- John the Baptist (*Yahya*) testified of Jesus — Q 3:38–41 (Luke 1:57–66)
- God preferred Jesus above the other messengers — Q 2:253 (Hebrews 1:1–3; Matthew 21:33–42)

- Jesus pronounced peace upon himself — Q 19:33 (John 13:13–17)
- God exalted Jesus — Q 2:253 (Philippians 2:9)
- Jesus is distinguished in the world — Q 3:45 (John 5:22)
- Jesus is near to God — Q 3:45 (John 14:7–9)
- God made Jesus blessed wherever he went — Q 19:31 (Luke 2:52)
- God made a covenant with his prophets (including Jesus) — Q 33:7 (Hebrews 6:13–18; Galatians 3:16)

The Followers of Jesus

- God's helpers are those who help Jesus — Q 3:52; Q 61:14 (1 John 2:23)
- Jesus had followers — Q 3:53 (John 3:26)
- God said to Jesus that he would make his followers higher than the unbelievers until Judgment Day — Q 3:55 (Ephesians 2:6; 2 Thessalonians 1:7–10)
- Jesus told God that the disciples were God's servants, and he could choose to punish or forgive them — Q 5:118 (John 17:6–11)

Jesus as the Fulfillment

- Jesus confirmed the Old Testament that was in his hands — Q 3:50; Q 5:46 (Deuteronomy 18:15; Luke 4:21; 16:17; Matthew 5:18; 15:1–6)

The Humanity of Jesus

- Jesus ate food — Q 5:75 (Luke 24:43)
- Jesus spoke to the people when an adult — Q 3:46; Q 5:110 (Matthew 5–7; John 14:10)
- God gave Jesus refuge — Q 23:50 (Luke 4:30)
- God is Jesus' Lord — Q 3:51; Q 5:117; Q 43:64 (John 20:17)
- God gave commandments to Jesus — Q 42:13 (Matthew 5–7)
- God commanded Jesus to pray and give alms while he remained alive (on earth) — Q 19:31 (John 17:1–6; 13:29; Luke 6:12; Matthew 19:21)

Jesus and Judgment Day

- On Judgment Day, Jesus will witness against those who did not believe in him before their death — Q 4:159 (John 5:22–23)

Jesus and His Miracles

- The child Jesus created a clay bird for the Jews and breathed life into it — Q 3:49; Q 5:110 (John 5:21; 20:22)
- Jesus gave sight to a man born blind — Q 3:49; Q 5:110 (John 9:1–12)
- Jesus healed a leper, raised the dead, and prophesied — Q 3:49; Q 5:110 (Matthew 11:5; Luke 7:22; John 11:43–44)
- Christ asked God to provide a meal from heaven — Q 5:112–114 (John 6:5–14, 27)
- God gave miracles to Jesus — Q 2:253 (Matthew 11:5; Acts 10:38)

The Names of Jesus

- *Christ* is Jesus' title — Q 4:157, 171 (John 4:25)
- His name is *Messiah,* Jesus, son of Mary — Q 3:45 (Matthew 1:21; Luke 2:11)
- Jesus is a spirit from God — Q 4:171; Q 21:91; Q 66:12 (Luke 1:35; Galatians 4:6)
- Jesus is a blessing from God — Q 19:21 (Luke 2:14)
- Jesus was a sign to all men — Q 21:91 (Luke 2:8–20)
- Christ was a witness over the people while with them — Q 5:117 (John 17:12–13, 26)

Jesus as a Prophet

- God aided Jesus with the Holy Spirit — Q 2:87, 253; Q 5:110 (Matthew 3:16; Luke 4:18; Acts 10:38)
- God caused Jesus to follow in the lineage of Jewish prophets — Q 5:46 (Matthew 21:33–41)
- Jesus was a prophet — Q 19:30 (Luke 11:49)

Jesus' Relationship to God

- God is *not* Christ the son of Mary — Q 5:17, 72 (1 Corinthians 8:6)
- God asked Jesus if he had told people to regard himself and Mary as two Gods in place of God — Q 5:116 (John 10:30; 17:21; Matthew 17:5)
- Jesus answered that he never said anything he had no right to say — Q 5:116 (John 14:10)

The Resurrection of Jesus

- God raised Jesus to himself — Q 4:158 (Mark 16:19)
- God plotted against the people's plot and won — Q 3:54 (Revelation 13:8; Matthew 20:17–19; Acts 3:15; 4:10; 1 Corinthians 2:8)
- The day that Jesus was raised was blessed — Q 19:33 (Isaiah 53:10–12)
- God said to Jesus that he would raise him up alive — Q 3:55; Q 19:33–34 (Acts 1:9; Luke 18:33)

Jesus and Revelations

- God gave Jesus the Bible — Q 19:30 (Luke 4:16–20)
- God revealed to the disciples of Jesus that they were to believe in God and in his messenger, Jesus — Q 5:110–111 (Mark 9:7; Luke 9:35)
- God gave Jesus the New Testament, in which is guidance and light — Q 5:46 (Luke 2:32)
- God taught Jesus the Bible and wisdom — Q 3:48; Q 5:110 (Luke 2:40)
- Jesus is greater than the law — Q 3:50 (Mark 7:14–20)
- Christ said that he brought the people wisdom — Q 43:63 (Matthew 13:1–52)

Jesus and Servanthood

- Jesus said that he was God's servant — Q 19:30 (John 20:17; Philippians 2:5–7)

- Jesus was not too arrogant to be God's servant — Q 4:172 (Philippians 2:6–7)
- Jesus is only a servant to whom God gave grace — Q 43:59 (Philippians 2:5–11)

Jesus Being Sinless

- Christ is sinless — Q 19:19 (Hebrews 7:26; 2 Corinthians 5:21; John 8:46)

Jesus as the Word

- Jesus is a saying of the truth — Q 19:34 (1 John 5:7–12, 20; 2:21; 1:1; 2 John 1)
- Jesus is a word from God — Q 3:45 (John 1:14)
- Jesus is God's word — Q 4:171 (John 1:1–3)
- God spoke/cast his word to Mary — Q 4:171 (Luke 1:35; John 1:14)

Muslims, Christians, and Jesus

Gaining Understanding and Building Relationships

Carl Medearis

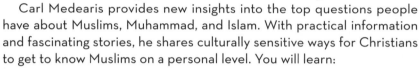

Despite growing numbers of Muslims and Christians living or working next to each other, major barriers remain. Not only do mistrust and fear get in the way, but so do misunderstandings. It doesn't have to be this way, however.

Carl Medearis provides new insights into the top questions people have about Muslims, Muhammad, and Islam. With practical information and fascinating stories, he shares culturally sensitive ways for Christians to get to know Muslims on a personal level. You will learn:

- How Islam's "Pillars of Faith" are lived out in today's world
- What the Qur'an says about women
- What Muslims think about the Bible and Jesus
- How to bring up spiritual matters in conversations
- And much more

Rather than focusing initially on the differences between Islam and Christianity, Medearis shows how common ground is the best foundation for friendships and for hearts turning to Jesus.

> *"I have experienced Carl's compassion for people firsthand. His wisdom and experience give him unique insight into... sharing Christ with the Muslim world."*
>
> —Ted Dekker, bestselling author of *Skin, House, and Three*

Softcover: 978-0-7642-0567-5

Available in stores and online!

Share Your Thoughts

With the Author: Your comments will be forwarded to the author when you send them to *zauthor@zondervan.com*.

With Zondervan: Submit your review of this book by writing to *zreview@zondervan.com*.

Free Online Resources at
www.zondervan.com

Zondervan AuthorTracker: Be notified whenever your favorite authors publish new books, go on tour, or post an update about what's happening in their lives at www.zondervan.com/authortracker.

Daily Bible Verses and Devotions: Enrich your life with daily Bible verses or devotions that help you start every morning focused on God. Visit www.zondervan.com/newsletters.

Free Email Publications: Sign up for newsletters on Christian living, academic resources, church ministry, fiction, children's resources, and more. Visit www.zondervan.com/newsletters.

Zondervan Bible Search: Find and compare Bible passages in a variety of translations at www.zondervanbiblesearch.com.

Other Benefits: Register yourself to receive online benefits like coupons and special offers, or to participate in research.

ZONDERVAN.com/
AUTHOR**TRACKER**
follow your favorite authors